COMPOSER SHOWCASE
HAL LEONARD STUDENT PIANO LIBRARY

Little Jazzers

NINE ORIGINAL PIANO SOLOS

BY JENNIFER WATTS

To Jay and Liam, my own little jazzers

T0070695

CONTENTS

ISBN 978-1-4950-5364-1

HAL•LEONARD®
CORPORATION
7777 W. BLUEMOUND RD. P.O. BOX 13819 MILWAUKEE, WI 53213

In Australia Contact:
Hal Leonard Australia Pty. Ltd.
4 Lentara Court
Cheltenham, Victoria, 3192 Australia
Email: ausadmin@halleonard.com.au

Visit Hal Leonard Online at
www.halleonard.com

My First Blues

By Jennifer Watts

Bluesy con moto (♩ = 120)

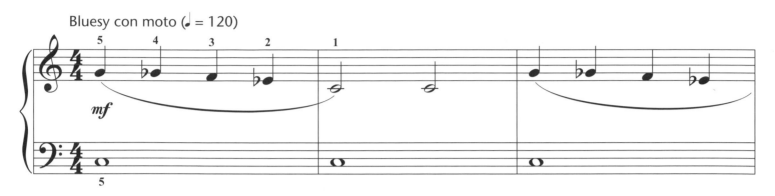

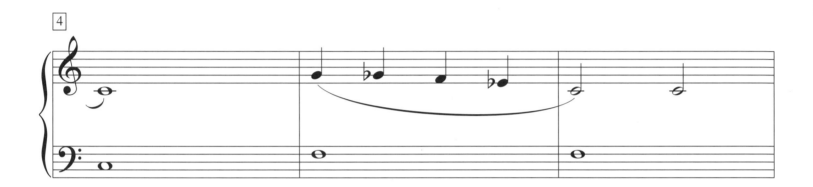

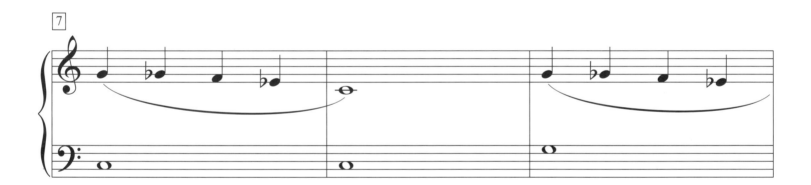

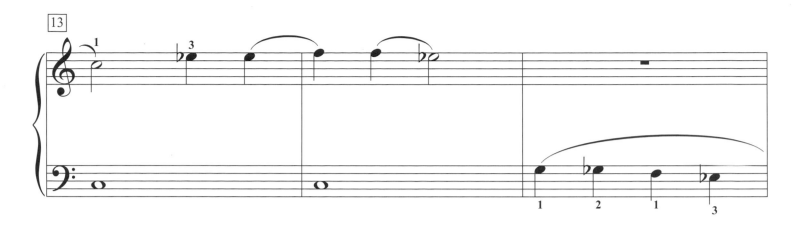

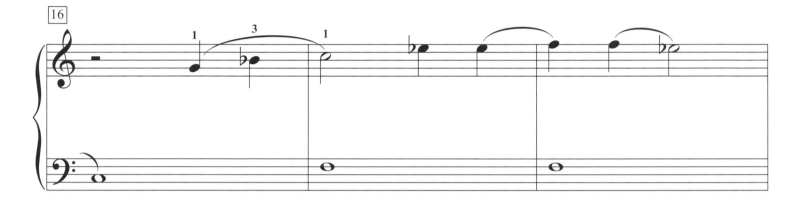

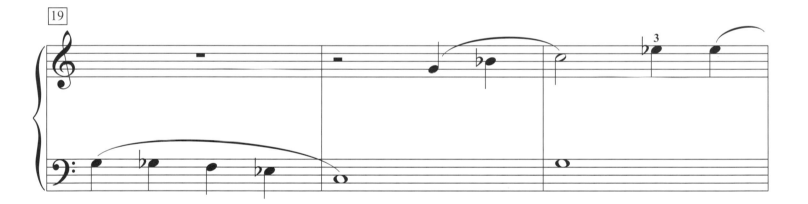

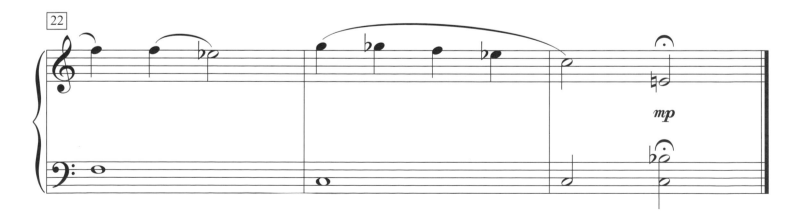

No Dessert Tonight

By Jennifer Watts

Sadly (♩ = c. 126)

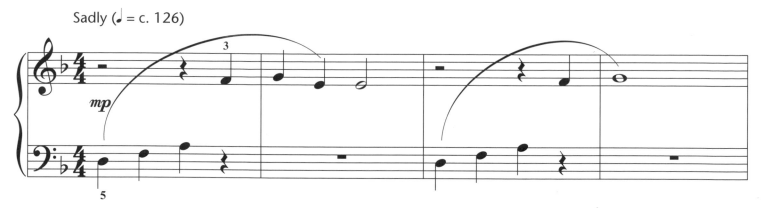

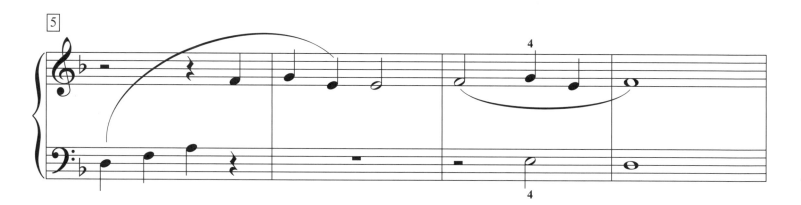

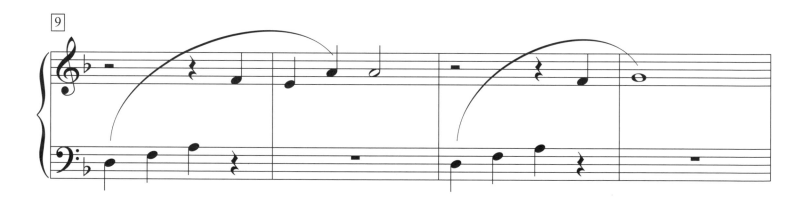

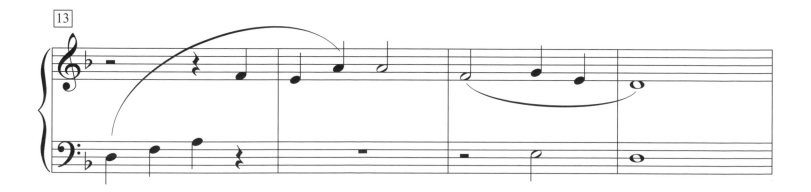

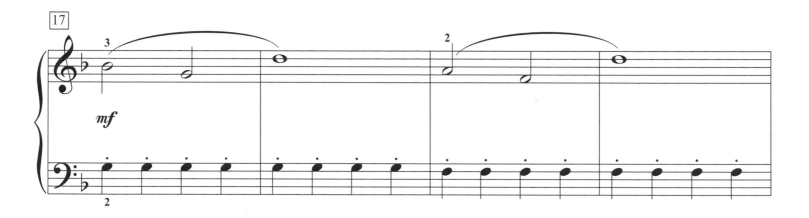

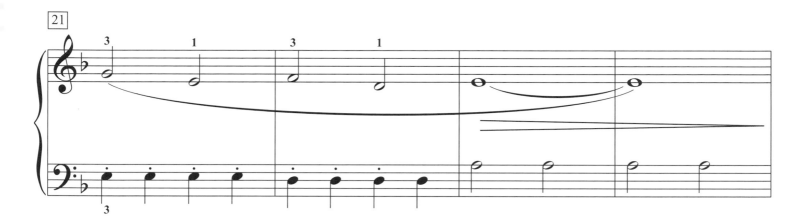

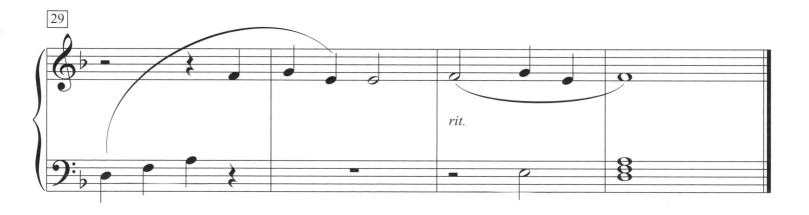

The Walrus Watusi

By Jennifer Watts

Lumbering Rock & Roll (♩ = c. 160)

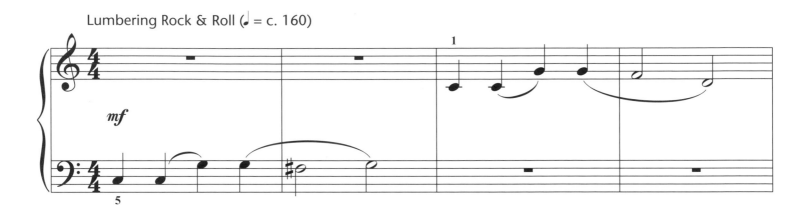

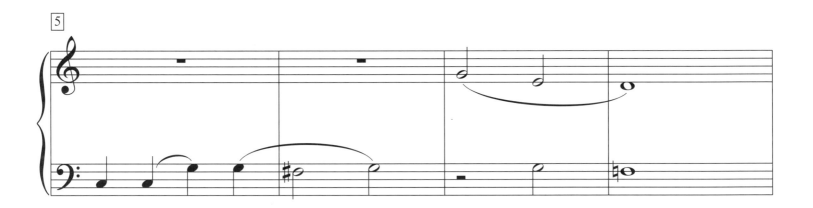

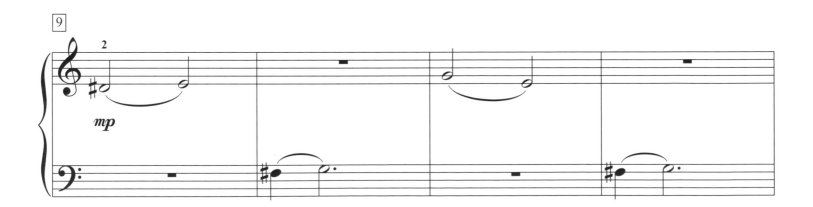

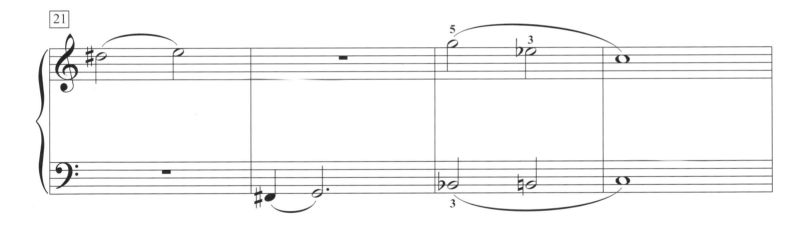

Charlie's Blues

By Jennifer Watts

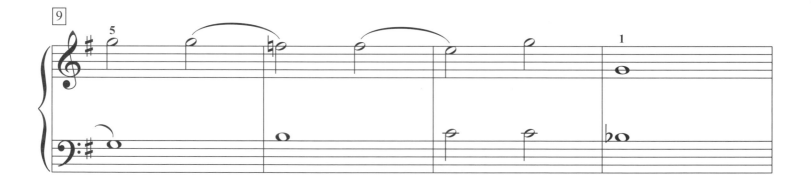

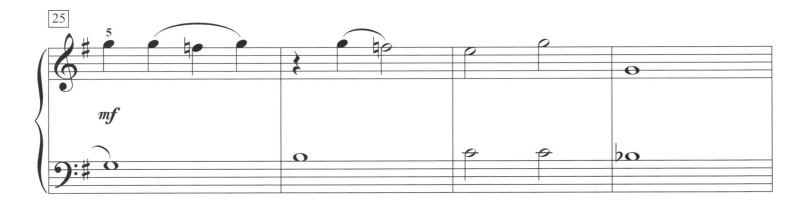

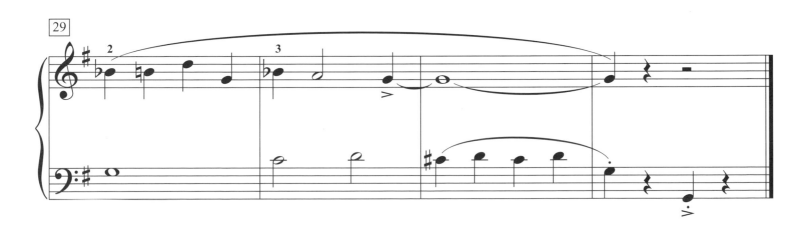

Blue Lullaby

By Jennifer Watts

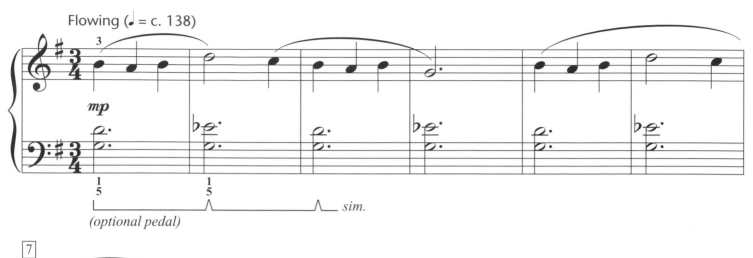

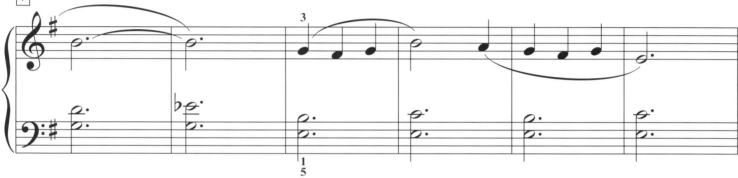

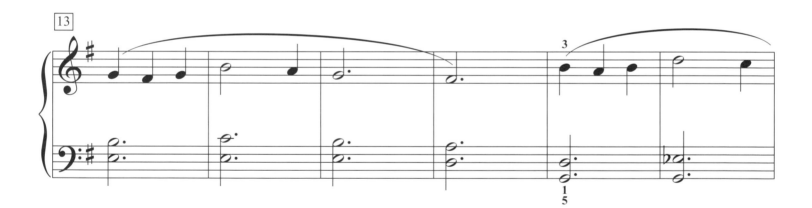

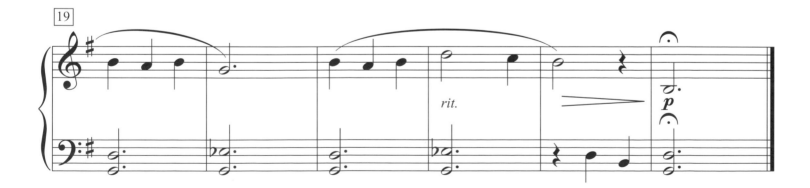

Orange Shoes Blues

By Jennifer Watts

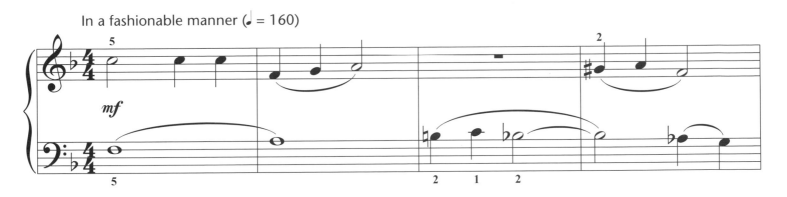

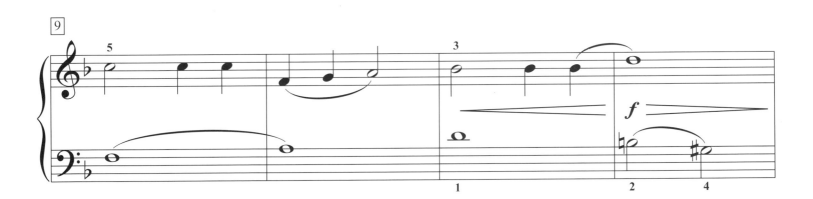

The Pajama Rag

By Jennifer Watts

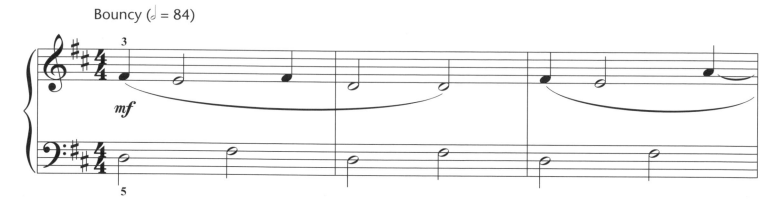

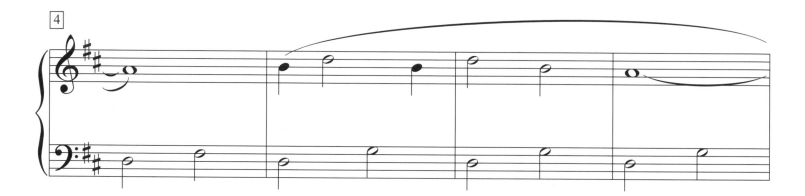

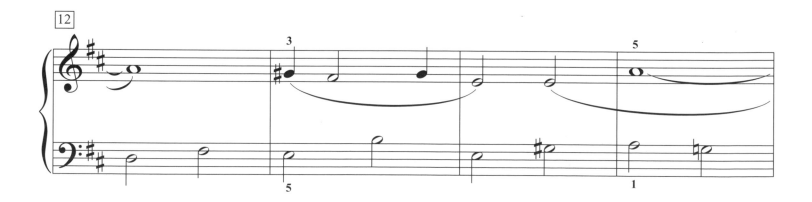

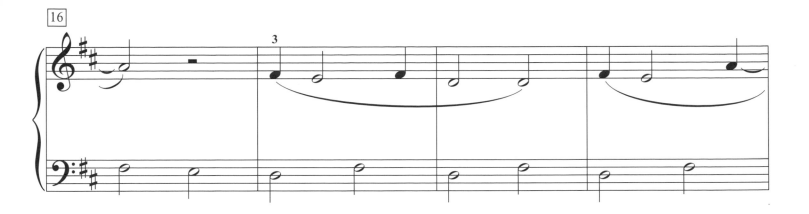

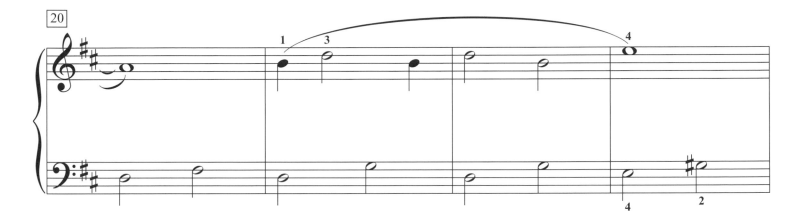

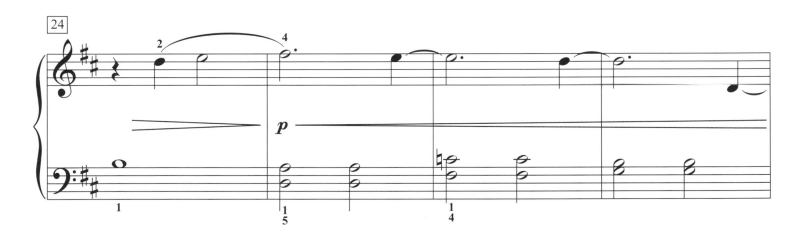

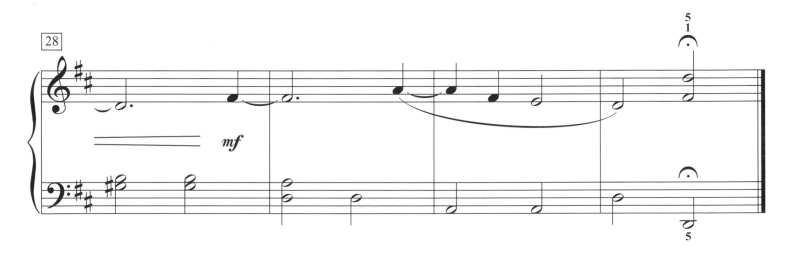

13

The Crooked Waltz

By Jennifer Watts

Andantino (♩ = 104)

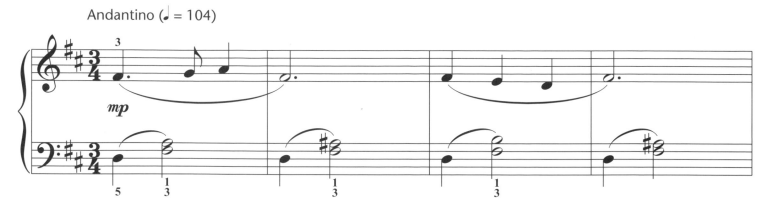

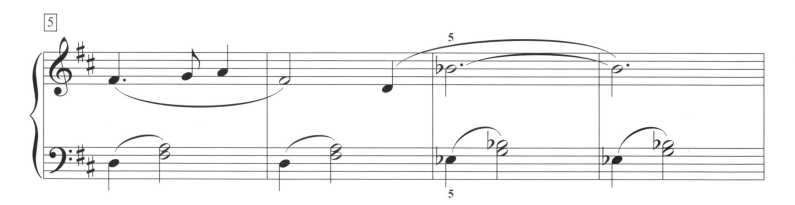

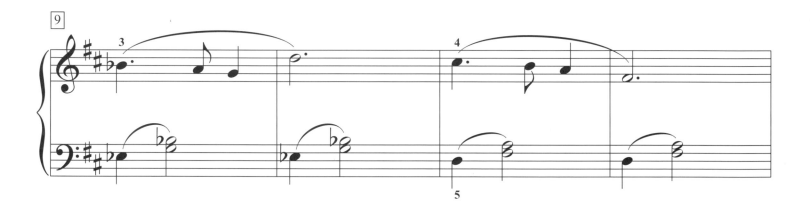

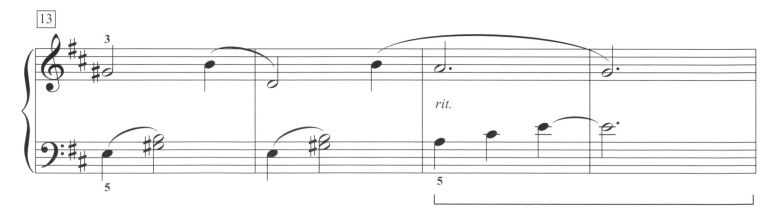

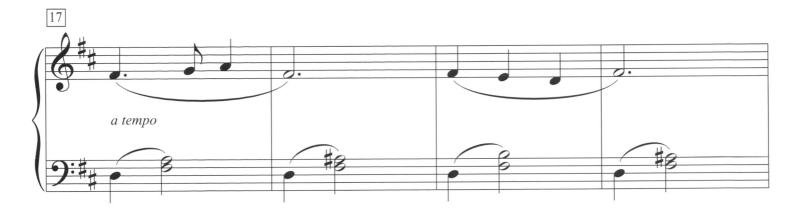

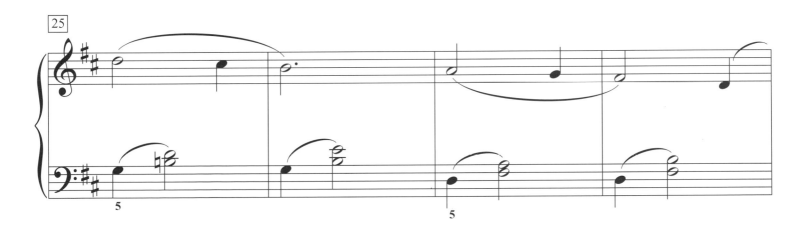

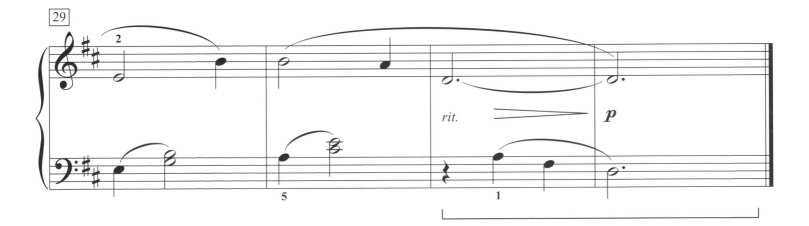

Basso Ostinato

By Jennifer Watts

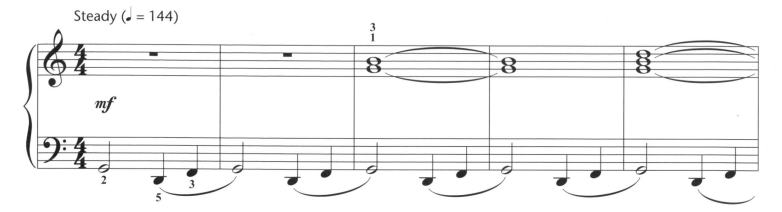

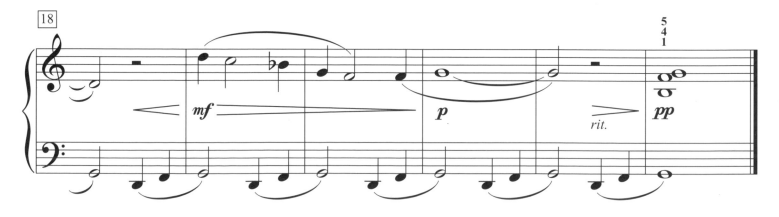